JUNIOR SURVIVAL LIBRARY

The Horse of the River

THE
HIPPOPOTAMUS

Malcolm Penny

ANGLIA
Television Limited

BOXTREE

Key to abbreviations

lb	pound
gm	gramme
kg	kilogram
in	inch
ft	feet
yd	yard
cm	centimetre
m	metre
km	kilometre
sq mile	square mile
sq km	square kilometre
kph	kilometres per hour
mph	miles per hour

First published in 1992 by Boxtree Limited
Copyright © 1992 Survival Anglia Limited
Text copyright © 1992 Malcolm Penny

Front jacket photograph:
Survival Anglia/Ian Wyllie
(Hippo in Botswana)
Back jacket photograph:
Survival Anglia/Bruce Davidson
(Hippo in N.E. Zaire)

Line drawing by Caroline Brett
Map by Raymond Turvey

A catalogue record for this book is available
from the British Library

ISBN 1–85283–345–9

Designed by Anita Ruddell
Typeset by Cambrian Typesetters, Frimley,
Surrey

Printed and bound in Italy
by OFSA s.p.a.

for Boxtree Limited,
36 Tavistock Street,
London WC2E 7PB

Contents

Unmistakeable hippo

The hippo's full name, hippopotamus, comes from two old Greek words, *hippos* meaning 'horse' and *potamos* meaning 'river'. *Hippopotamus* is how the Romans spelled it, and it is the hippo's scientific name to this day. The first part of the name is wrong: hippos are not closely related to horses. The second part shows that the Greeks knew the animals at first hand: hippos most often live in shallow, slow-flowing rivers, as well as in still pools and swamps less than 1.5 m (5 ft) deep.

The bulky-bodied hippo is adapted to spending a large part of its time supported by water.

A hippo's nose, eyes and ears are still above water when its body is submerged.

The other part of a common hippo's scientific name is *amphibius*, which means that it lives partly on land and partly in water. The main reason for the hippo's distinctive shape is that it is an **aquatic** animal. Because its weight is supported most of the time in water it can afford to be rounded and heavy with a small surface area in relation to its volume. This means that it loses heat only slowly in the water.

The hippo spends a large part of each night feeding on land and, although its legs look rather weak for its bulk, it can run quite fast for short distances. Underwater, hippos move with surprising ease and grace, often tiptoeing along the bottom like huge, tubby ballet dancers.

A hippo's sense organs are placed on top of its head, all at one level, so that when the rest of its body is submerged it can still see, hear, breathe and sniff the breeze. When it dives below the surface a hippo closes its slit-shaped nostrils and folds its ears inwards to keep the water out. When it surfaces again it flaps its ears briskly, shaking the water out of them, so that it can listen as well as look out for danger.

The most striking thing about a hippo's appearance is its huge gaping jaws, the lower one armed with two large yellowish tusks. It can open its jaws very wide indeed. This may be used merely as a threatening gesture to another hippo but adults do often fight and even occasionally kill each other. As we shall see, hippos are very lazy animals with a slow and apparently peaceful way of life but at the same time they have evolved as fighters with fearsome weapons and armour to protect themselves against others of their kind.

Facts and Figures

Name: Hippopotamus amphibius

Length of head and body:
  male 3-5 m (9 ft 8 in-16 ft 5 in)
  female 3-4.3 m (9 ft 5 in-14 ft)

Weight:
  male 506-3,200 kg (0.5-3.1 tons)
  female 655-2,344 kg (0.64-2.2 tons)

Height: 1.5-1.65 m (5 ft-5 ft 4 in)

Tail: 40 cm (15.7 in)

The earliest hippos

The fossils of many animals, such as horses, show gradual changes over millions of years until an unfamiliar early form becomes the animal we know today. 50 million years ago horses were no bigger than dogs, but we can follow the stages by which they reached their present form. Hippos are different: they seem to have come long ago from the same ancestors as pigs, but the route they followed

To make an effective challenge in water, a hippo's tusks are in its lower jaw.

is a mystery.

A few hippo teeth have been found in rocks about 25 million years old, but the next oldest fossil hippo is not much more than 10 million years old, and already very similar to modern hippos.

At about that time there were hippos of many different types, some of them more lightly built and with much longer legs than modern hippos. Their teeth show that they ate a softer diet, perhaps of leaves and flowering plants rather than grass, and their feet, with four toes and no hoof to protect them, suggest that they must have walked mostly on soft, damp ground like the hippos of today.

The first hippos probably lived in forests, like many modern pigs. However, it seems that they soon moved out of the trees and into water, where they **evolved** their distinctive jaws and teeth because of their way of fighting.

Pigs fight by biting at each other with wide-open mouths, slashing with tusks in their upper jaws. If early hippos fought in the same way in water they would have had to hold their heads well up to avoid drowning. Thus, they had to evolve tusks in their lower jaw, not the upper, for defence as well as attack.

The tusks grew large and very strong to withstand the clashing of face-to-face challenges and they grew further apart to offer the widest possible defence. The gape of the jaws became wider as well, to keep the soft nose and upper lip out of the way of the fight. Modern hippos can open their jaws to form an angle of nearly 150° when they are fighting.

There are only two modern species of hippo. One of them still lives, like its ancestors, deep in the forest: it is the mysterious pygmy hippo of West Africa. Much rarer than its larger relative, this timid animal hides in dense thickets to avoid its enemy, man.

A hippo's broad feet, without hooves, are designed for walking on soft ground.

HIPPO DISTRIBUTION

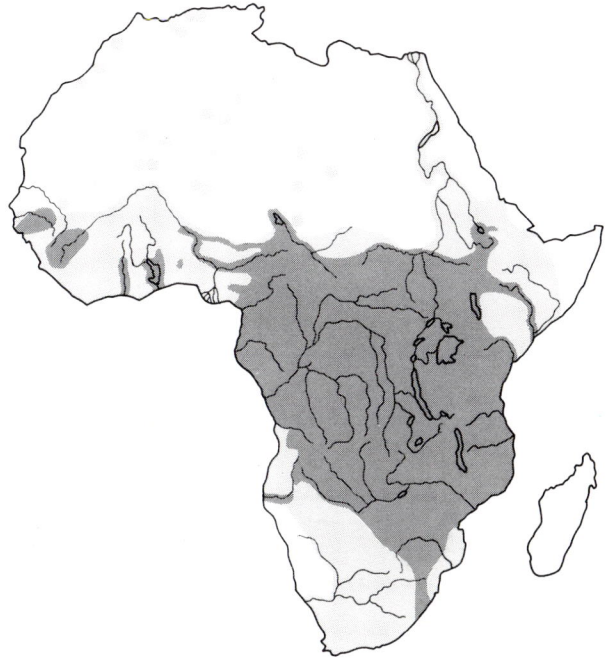

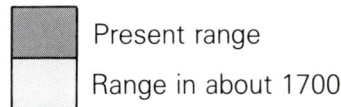

▨	Present range
☐	Range in about 1700

Hippos were once widespread in Africa. Nowadays, due to persecution by man and changes in their habitat, they are very scarce in most rivers outside eastern Africa.

The pygmy hippo

The pygmy hippo's scientific name is *Choeropsis liberiensis*, which means 'the pig-like animal that lives in Liberia'. It is a good description: a pygmy hippo is not much bigger than a pig and it is found only in rivers and swamps in the remaining dense **primary forests** of Liberia, where it has become very rare. It is one-third the size of a common hippo. Fully grown, its body length is about 1.5 m (5 ft). It stands about 85 cm (33.5 in) tall and it weighs between 180 and 260 kg (396–572 lb).

The pygmy hippo's body is almost completely hairless with tufts only on the ears and the tip of the tail and a bristly moustache on the upper lip. It is more **streamlined** than a common hippo with short, sturdy legs and a relatively smaller head. It can open its jaws nearly as wide but its tusks are not as large. They serve a similar purpose, as weapons as well as for feeding. They are very sharp and

Pygmy hippos survive today only in dense riverside forests.

can inflict serious injuries when two animals fight.

Pygmy hippos feed on aquatic plants as well as grass and bushes on land, moving about in small family groups. They are very shy, running to water when they are disturbed by humans. They often use paths which burrow through dense **bush** where their enemies cannot follow. They have every reason to be timid because they are still hunted for food. Hunting is the main reason why they are so rare.

The number surviving in the wild is not known; they are rarely seen and are usually thought to be in danger of **extinction**. However, since pygmy hippos were first captured and brought to Europe in 1912,

The pygmy hippo gets its scientific name from its pig-like appearance.

they have proved to settle down well in zoos, both there and in North America. They become tame and are quite easy to breed. Consequently, and perhaps sadly, more is known about their breeding behaviour in captivity than their general behaviour in the wild. One old male lived in Basel Zoo, in Switzerland, until he was 33 years old.

Common hippos usually give birth in the water but pygmy mothers-to-be, at least in captivity, must be kept on land because their babies cannot swim when they are born but have to learn as they grow up. Soon, they are able to feed from their mothers underwater.

A day in the life of a lazy animal

Hippos lead slow, placid lives most of the time, spending the day either sunning themselves on a mudbank or **wallowing** in mud or shallow water. They prefer places where there is little or no current, like the banks of broad rivers or pools in swamps. Where one river flows into another there are often suitable mudbanks providing gently sloping beaches into the water.

Hippos need sunshine to keep warm when the water is cold and water to cool them down during the hot, dry season. They need to wallow regularly to prevent them drying out in the sun: the outer layer of their skin is very thin and easily loses water through **evaporation**.

Mothers and young stay close together, keeping out of the way of the large males who often fight during the day. A mother hippo defends her young fiercely at all times and if danger threatens they cluster round her for protection.

When it is quite dark, at about 8 or 9 o'clock, hippos leave the water and climb

Wallowing keeps hippos cool and their skin supple.

When the weather is mild, hippos spend part of the day resting on land.

onto the bank to feed. Although their legs look rather weak, they can climb steep banks and they can run for short distances at over 30 kph (18.6 mph). Once on land, family groups walk in single file along regular paths to their favourite feeding places. No hippo will walk more than 10 km (6 miles) to find food and they usually travel no more than 3–5 km (2–3 miles). They use their horny lips to grip the short grass, tearing or uprooting it with a swing of the head.

Feeding does not take very long. Although hippos look very fat they eat surprisingly little. Cattle eat about one-fortieth (2.5%) of their body weight every day but hippos need only a little over a hundredth (1%). It takes them only a few hours to eat their fill and return to the water's edge or into the water. During the rainy season some hippos spend the day in temporary pools or in wet vegeta-tion away from the river to save themselves a walk the next night.

In long dry spells hippos can go without feeding for weeks at a time so long as they can find a muddy place to wallow. At times like this, moving little in order to save energy, they are living off their fat.

Slow digestion is efficient digestion

A hippo's stomach is divided into three chambers. The dry, tough grass, which is only roughly chewed, is **fermented** in the stomach chambers. This process makes good use of the food but it is very slow: the stomach can hold 2 days' worth of food and digestion does not start until more than 12 hours after the hippo has finished a meal.

11

Eating the environment

The hippo's way of feeding, often tearing grass up by the roots, can be very destructive. Where hippo populations are large and crowded there is a risk that the feeding grounds might be stripped bare.

In Uganda, in 1958, the population of hippos round the shores of Lake Edward was grossly overcrowded. The damage to the pasture was so great that other grazing animals had to move away in search of food. At that time there were two hippos feeding on each hectare (2.5 acres) of grass and local biologists estimated that they needed at least ten times as much space. Finally, the authorities decided that many of the hippos had to be shot to allow the pasture to recover.

Population control of this kind is not an ideal way to keep the numbers steady, especially in a National Park, but with few **predators** to control their numbers and hunting by local people banned, the hippos were in danger of completely wrecking their part of the Park.

Hippos and catfish crowd together in a drying waterhole.

Another effect of over-grazing by hippos was noticed in Ruwenzori National Park, also in Uganda. Because they graze so thoroughly in their favourite feeding areas they leave no dead grass to catch fire in the dry season. This allows small trees to grow, forming thickets where there was once pasture. Eventually, the hippos have to move on because they have nothing to eat.

Along one river in Zambia, where hippos are now rare, dense thickets on the banks show where they used to feed until they destroyed their own food supply. This is a form of natural population control which has been going on since hippos evolved.

Where they are not too crowded, hippos may have the opposite effect – actually improving the pasture for themselves and other animals.

Although it might seem a strange statement to find in a natural history book, hippo meat is good to eat, as Africans have known for a long time. If proper studies were made to find which animals a growing population could best spare, the conclusion might be that exploiting hippos as food for local people is a logical option.

Hippos can damage their grazing places by tearing up grass by the roots.

Dancing underwater

A hippo's legs have been described as 'designed for sitting down'. Although they can move long distances over land, especially in the wet season when they may follow rivers or **colonise** small temporary ponds, hippos spend most of their time taking their weight off their feet.

In water, where their weight is **buoyed up**, hippos move with grace and agility with their forelegs folded back against their body. They have a long supple back and swim with kicking movements of their hind legs. Walking delicately on the bottom, bounding gently along, they disturb the mud as little as possible.

Hippos can stay underwater for longer periods the older they are. Babies can stay down for less than 30 seconds. They can feed from their mothers on land or underwater but they always behave as if they are submerged. Even when it is sucking on land,

Underwater, hippos swim or move lightly and gracefully on tiptoe.

Labio are small fish which groom hippos by removing dead skin while they sleep.

a baby hippo closes its nostrils and folds its ears, pausing every few sucks to raise its head, open its nostrils, waggle its ears and take a deep breath.

Older hippos can stay underwater for longer, from about 2 minutes for young ones to 4–5 minutes for adults. When they are alarmed they tend to stay underwater for longer than when they are at ease.

When they come to the surface, hippos blow water from their nostrils but often keep their heads down at first so that their eyes and ears are the only other parts showing.

Hippos usually drop their dung in the water. As we shall see later, passing dung on land is the privilege of the senior males.

An important result of dropping dung in the water is the enormous fertility of ponds and rivers regularly used by hippos. By feeding on land and leaving their droppings in the water they transfer energy to the water from the land. Fish find plenty of food there, eating the plants which grow in the rich water, and insects also feed on the plants or the dung itself. One type of fish, called Labio, specialises in grooming hippos, removing dead skin and **parasites** from them as they doze in the water.

Travels in rainy weather

When the rains are well established, hippos may wander long distances from their usual riverside haunts. This is not because they are looking for food - there is plenty at this time of year - but it may be a means of exploring to find new places to live. One young female walked over 1,600 km (994 miles) in South Africa before she was found again and shot.

Mating and birth

Male hippos become **sexually mature** between 4 and 11 years old and females between 7 and 15. The females will probably breed before the males because males have to fight with their seniors for the right to mate. **Dominant** males defend their favourite bathing places and even the paths which lead to them; they always try to keep as close as they can to where the females gather with their young. Junior males, because they are smaller and lighter than the seniors, find it very hard to fight their way in.

Mating takes place in the water, usually at the end of one of the two dry seasons, in February and August. This is when the hippos are crowded closest together and when the females are most receptive. When

A male will soon overpower the lighter female in their courtship tussles.

the male has found a female **in season** he chases her until she turns and faces him, clashing jaws in a ritual struggle. Because he is much heavier she soon gives in and the male pushes her underwater to mate with her.

The young are born about 8 months later. The timing of mating means that the babies appear during the rains when there is plenty of grass for their mothers to eat.

Birth takes place on land or in shallow water, often in a favoured place used by most of the females in the group. Twins are very rare, appearing in only one birth in every hundred and fifty.

The baby hippo may weigh between 25 and 45 kg (55–99 lb). It can walk almost at once, but not very far. The mother stays close to her baby, ready to defend it against any danger. Later, it will follow her closely wherever she goes. If it begins to stray she punishes it by butting it with her head.

The baby feeds from its mother for nearly a year although it can chew grass after only a month and will begin to graze at about 5 months.

How a grazing animal sucks milk

A hippo's mouth is adapted to eat short grass which it grips between its horny lips. It is not well suited to sucking. A baby hippo feeds from its mother by using its tongue held against the roof of its mouth, to hold the teat.

Once the baby can walk well, at about 7 weeks old, its mother may allow as many as three other young hippos to join them. They follow her in single file as she walks between the water and the grazing place. They are not necessarily her earlier young: females seem prepared to look after any young hippos. The young need looking after because they are growing up in a very violent society.

Hippos walk in line, the baby with its mother, to the feeding grounds.

Growing up in a violent society

Young hippos, especially males, fight from an early age. If two of about the same size and weight meet, on land or in the water, they challenge each other with wide-open mouths and begin clashing their tusks and pushing. If one is bigger, the smaller hippo will usually turn and move away; sometimes, on land, he will show submission by lying down instead.

Females with young tend to stay away from the main group of hippos, especially during the mating season, because of the danger from males looking for mates. Predators are less of a threat because the mother is so fierce in defending her young.

At the first sign of danger the young hippos gather round the female, even though she may not be their mother. This behaviour continues into later life: if a group of adult hippos is disturbed they huddle closer together in the water.

The youngest hippo in the group is closest to the female (who almost certainly *is* its mother) and the others take their place in order of size. All are subject to strict discipline. If they start to wander or stop to play on the way to the feeding ground the

A baby stays close to its mother until it is big enough to look after itself.

female will hit them with her head or even bite them until they get into line. To avoid further punishment they lie down – another piece of juvenile behaviour which will be carried on into later life.

Larger groups of young form when their mothers move away to mate, or perhaps just to feed quietly for a while. These '**creches**' are looked after by one or two older females, often called 'aunts'. The 'aunts' will fight just as fiercely for their nieces and nephews as if they were their own offspring.

Sometimes the groups of young are attacked by a large male. The females in charge are

A dense school of hippos in the Luangwa River, Zambia.

usually able to drive the male away, even though he is much bigger. This is because males usually fight according to a set of rules, involving clashing and parrying blows, while females – with the lives of their young at stake – tend to aim deliberate bites or even ignore the rules altogether and attack from the side or more than one at a time.

Even though the males follow rules of fighting they are often seriously hurt or even killed in their battles for dominance.

The rules of the fight

A dominant male hippo continually shows his seniority by showering his rivals with dung, wagging his tail violently until the spray travels 1 m (3.2 ft) or more. The dung has a strong smell by which other hippos can identify who produced it. A good spraying may be enough to convince a rival that it is not worth fighting. Only dominant males produce dung on land, as a way of maintaining their dominance. Most hippos will spray in water as part of their frequent fights.

However, spraying is often not enough. The next step in a fight is the challenge. A male rears up out of the water, opening his mouth wide to show the bright pink inside, and honks loudly. If the challenge is accepted by a nearby male both raise their rumps out of the water and spray dung into the air. The heads of both contestants are often covered with a red **secretion** from their sweat glands which makes them look as if they are bleeding.

Then the hippos attack, crashing their lower jaws together with great force. The tusks meet so violently that they are often chipped. Like the antlers of a stag, the tusks are designed to catch those of an opponent and prevent him striking the head or chest. Hippos have no armour on the front part of their body.

The push-of-war that follows may go on

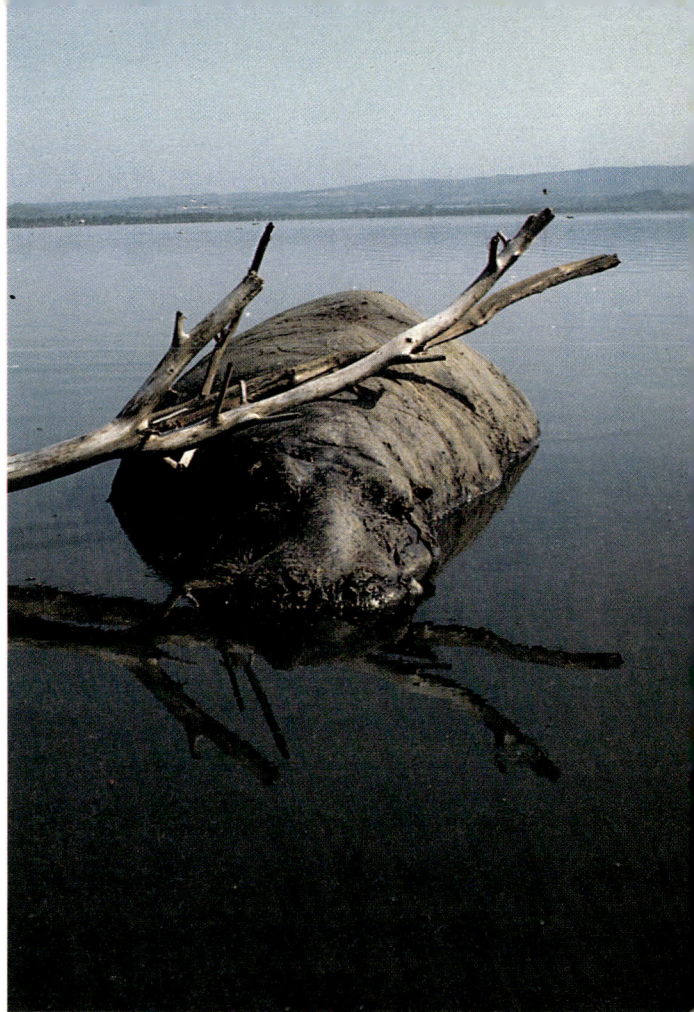

In spite of the rituals of the fight, hippos may be killed in combat.

for an hour or more with frequent clashes and occasional periods of rest; but as soon as one begins to lose ground, the fight is over.

On land, the loser sometimes lies down in the childish gesture of submission, but more often he turns tail and moves away. This is not as risky as it sounds because the rump, as well as the back and sides of a hippo are covered in tough skin which might be as much as 6 cm (2.3 in) thick.

In spite of the rules of the fight and their armoured rear ends, hippos are often badly wounded, and sometimes killed, in fights.

Younger males **spar** amongst themselves rather than fighting. In doing so they prepare for the more serious fights which they will have to face later in life.

First Aid before being hurt?

The red secretion which covers fighting males may be a form of natural antiseptic to help heal any wounds received during a fight. Open wounds would otherwise become septic very easily in the warm, contaminated water where most fights take place.

Senior males fight to be near the females in the breeding season.

Enemies of the hippo

The greatest natural danger to young hippos, especially in a crowded population, comes not from predators but from adult male hippos. When a male wants to mate with a female he regards any other animal in the water nearby as an enemy, including the female's smallest offspring which normally stays very close to its mother. Many young hippos are killed at such a time if they are with their mothers and not safely guarded by aunts when they group together in a creche

Lions feeding on a buffalo with hyaenas in attendance.

A hippo badly wounded by a lion. It died shortly after this photograph was taken.

with other youngsters.

When 3,000 hippos were shot in a National Park in Uganda, in 1958, the number of young hippos less than 1 year old went up from 5% to 14% in the next 7 years. The animals which were shot were mainly the larger members of the group, most of them males. Once they were gone, the babies survived nearly three times as well.

Lions and hyaenas kill young hippos if they can catch them away from their mothers. Lions have been known to attack adult hippos, though they find it difficult to kill them because of their armoured skin. One biologist saw a group of lions kill two hippos by rolling them over on to their backs and biting their vulnerable chests and throats.

Humans have killed hippos for thousands of years for food with spears or in **pitfall traps**. In the old days this level of human predation did no harm to the hippo population.

When Europeans arrived with guns they began to shoot hippos for sport, just because they were big, sometimes fierce, animals and rather hard to kill cleanly. This type of 'big game shooting' is now regarded by most people as barbaric and very few such 'sportsmen' still go hunting.

As the human population grew, however, a much more serious threat came from the spread of agriculture. Hippos can damage growing crops on their nightly feeding expeditions and they are unpredictable and often dangerous if a human takes them by surprise. Because of this, they are being wiped out or seriously reduced in numbers wherever humans want the land for farming.

23

Less wild Africa, fewer hippos

The two main things hippos need from their environment are permanent water and grass to eat. They can live on high ground up to about 700 m (2,295 ft). In theory, there is nowhere in the whole of Africa, outside the great deserts and a few mountainsides, that is unsuitable for hippos.

About 4,000 years ago, hippos were so numerous in Egypt that they were considered

This orphan hippo was brought up as a pet in Africa and became quite tame.

Farmers often take over the hippos' habitat, sometimes killing them to protect their crops.

a plague. They were hunted and killed because of the damage they did to crops along the banks of the Nile.

The Romans used hippos as they used other large animals from Africa, in their circuses. A Roman circus was very different from those of our own time. Instead of clowns they had gladiators who entertained the crowd by killing, or being killed by, wild animals and each other. Their victims, the first hippos to be seen in Europe, came from Egypt and possibly also further east in the country then known as Palestine. The last hippos in Egypt were wiped out by 1815. South of the Sahara there were hippos all over Africa, even in 1700.

The growth of the human population of Africa, with the consequent increase in hunting and the spread of farming, was already reducing the hippo's numbers when European colonisation began. What followed was a catastrophe for hippos, especially in the south, as well as for several other large 'game' animals. As we have seen, hunters with rifles killed many hippos for sport but the main reason for the slaughter was to clear farmland of these large and, to the farmers, potentially dangerous animals. There are now no hippos in most parts of South Africa.

Today, the only large populations of hippos survive in National Parks and other reserves. They live in the eastern Congo and in south-western Uganda, where there are 2,500 in Queen Elizabeth Park – half the country's total. There are some on the northern shore of Lake Victoria and along some of the rivers flowing into the southern end of Lake Tanganyika. Kenya has only 5,000 left because farmers have shot them to protect their crops and themselves and local hunters have killed them for meat and ivory.

The future of the hippo as a wild animal of Africa seems very uncertain.

A trade in hippos?

A hippo's tusks are made of ivory. They can weigh over 3 kg (6.6 lb) each, though the largest are often damaged by the owner's lifetime of fighting.

Although the 1989 **CITES** agreement reduced the market for elephants' tusks and saved a lot of elephants from poaching, there is still a demand for ivory. The largest single use of ivory is in Japan where it is carved into the personal seals which businessmen use to sign letters. To satisfy this market many hippos are being killed.

One country where hippos are still said to be common is Tanzania where the Selous National Park holds a large population. There is a plan to kill 2,000 hippos a year, in the Selous, for their ivory. The meat will be

Every new carved tusk means that another hippo has been killed.

6,000 elephant tusks, worth £3 million, were burnt in Keyna.

sold locally or dried to make **biltong** for export. The skin will be made into leather in a new tannery to be built nearby. Even the bones will have a use, being ground up and sold to gardeners as bone meal.

This plan seems to suit everyone (except the hippos). It will provide employment for local people and an income of over a million dollars a year to the Government which will be used to maintain wildlife reserves. Scientists are sure that the hippo population of the Selous can withstand the loss.

However, there are drawbacks to the plan. If hippo ivory becomes valuable on the international market, hippos will be worth poaching. Also, regular **culling** will change the structure of the hippo population in the Park.

The hunters will choose the animals with the biggest tusks – that is, the senior males. This may well improve the survival of small hippos during the mating season but it will quickly make the culling less worthwhile. It takes a hippo up to 10 years to grow full-sized tusks, yet there seems little chance of any hippo living that long in a population in which the biggest males are shot every year.

If hippos are to live on in Africa, for the amazement of people yet unborn and indeed for their own sake as animals, there may have to be a different plan for their survival.

Hippos for ever?

Hippos have very little future on land which has been taken over by people. The human population of Africa is growing so fast that soon there will be little or no land outside the National Parks which is not in permanent cultivation and so there will be nowhere else for hippos to live.

The pygmy hippo may already be on the way to extinction, though there are parts of the deepest forests of Liberia where some individuals might escape the hunters and linger on unseen for many years. Its future as a species seems to lie in zoos, where it has been breeding steadily since the first five animals were brought to Europe in 1912.

It is a sad thought that the same fate might lie in store for the common hippo. It, too, breeds quite readily in captivity and is hunted in the wild – even, as we have seen, in at least one National Park.

Most African countries support their

The strength of hippos should be respected rather than feared.

National Parks because they bring in tourists. Most also run the Parks on the animals' terms. If people want to see large, dangerous animals in their natural habitat they must be prepared to take the risk of unexpectedly close encounters – they may, perhaps, be watching large hippos from a small boat.

By their very nature the Parks are enclosed to keep the animals in and poachers out. We have seen how easily a population of hippos can destroy its food supply by over-grazing. It is not hard to imagine the situation where the hippos in a Park have eaten themselves out of house and home and have nowhere else to go to find food. Then the authorities will have a difficult decision to make: to feed the hippos artificially or to cull them – reducing the population to one that the habitat can support and, incidentally, to earn some welcome foreign currency.

Hippo farms may come to replace culling as a source of ivory and meat. The National Parks will surely act as a reservoir of hippos into the foreseeable future. However, the day has gone when this magnificent creature ruled unchallenged in the swamps and along the riverbanks of Africa.

Hippos should be left in peace in the rivers where they have always lived.

Glossary

Aquatic Living in water.

Biltong Strips of meat dried in the air for eating later.

Buoyed up Supported by the water, partly floating.

Bush Wild, uncultivated country.

CITES The Convention on International Trade in Endangered Species, an agreement to control the movement of rare animals and plants from one country to another.

Colonisation People or animals from somewhere else settling into a new place.

Contaminated Dirty, full of bacteria or germs.

Creche A gathering of young animals, usually looked after by one or more adults.

Culling Killing in order to control population size.

Dominant A dominant animal is senior to all the others in its group.

Evaporation When water evaporates it disappears into the air. The vapour is sometimes visible as steam.

Evolved In the process of evolution, animals change gradually over thousands or millions of years until they are better suited to their environment.

Extinction The death of the last of a particular species of animal, so that it has gone forever.

Fermented Rotted by the action of bacteria or yeast.

In season A female animal which is ready to mate is said to be 'in season'.

Parasites Animals or plants which get their food from others without killing them. Fleas and leeches are blood-sucking parasites.

Pitfall trap A hole dug in the ground and covered with leaves or branches to trap an animal.

Predator An animal which kills others for food.

Primary forests Forests in which the trees have never been felled.

Secretion A liquid produced by glands inside an animal or in its skin.

Sexually mature Old enough to mate and produce young.

Spar Pretend to fight.

Streamlined Shaped so as to move easily through air or water.

Wallowing Lying in water or soft mud to keep clean and cool.

Index

The entries in **bold** are illustrations.

Picture Acknowledgements

The publishers would like to thank the
Survival Anglia picture library
and the following photographers for the use
of photographs on the pages listed:

Cindy Buxton 23; Bob Campbell 17, 18;
Bruce Davidson 4, 6, 11, 23, 25, 26; Deeble/
Stone 29; Nick Gordon 8; Chris Knights 13;
Andrew Park 6; Dieter Plage 20; Dieter &
Mary Plage 10; Alan Root 15; Jean Root 12,
18, 22, 25, 27; Alan & Joan Root 15, 28;
Crispin Sadler 16; Maurice Tibbles 9; Colin
Willock 5.

With thanks to Kathryn Shreeve for her
valuable help and picture research.

About the author

Malcolm Penny has a B.Sc. Hons degree in Zoology from Bristol University in England. He trained as a schoolteacher, but soon became involved in conservation. After working in the Indian Ocean for the International Council for Bird Preservation and the Royal Society, he moved to the Wildfowl and Wetlands Trust. Since 1973 he has been a producer of natural history programmes for Survival Anglia, the internationally-renowned wildlife film-makers based in Norwich, England.